Chloe and Sam are going to bed

Author: Anna Monica Cooper

3-6 years

This is The Second Book in The series about Chloe and Sam

CHLOE AND SAM ARE GOING TO BED

This is the second book in the series about Chloe and Sam.

A sweet little girl named Chloe and her best friend, her beloved black and white dog named Sam, love the adventures they share together every day.

Like many children, they hate to get ready for bed because they'd rather stay up and play.

This story follows them as they go through their bedtime routine and head off to a land filled with sweet dreams as they discover maybe bedtime isn't so bad after all.

**Spending the weekend with children?
We have a solution!**

We wanted to show our appreciation
that you support our work so We've put
together a free gift for you!

Here are our best ideas for spending an
interesting time with your children.

Just visit the link above to download it now:

jmpublisher.com/e-book

We know you will love this gift!
Thanks!

A sweet little girl Chloe

And her beloved dog Sam

Fill their days with adventures

And all the fun that they can.

Their hours are full of laughter,

They never want the day to end.

What could possibly be better

Than spending time with your best friend?

Having fun playing outside
Is what Chloe and Sam do best.
They dread coming in for dinner,
Because soon bedtime will be next.

Eating dinner with the family,
At the table they take a seat.
Dear Sam can always be found
Laying right at Chloe's feet.

Then it's off to the bath tub.
Splashing with bubbles and toys,
Getting clean can be fun too.
But bedtime's not one of those joys.

Time to pick out the pajamas

That Miss Chloe would like to wear.

She loves her fuzzy slippers,

But still thinks bedtime is unfair.

Brushing her teeth to make them shine

On the schedule is what's next.

Chloe's starting to feel sleepy,

It seems her parents know what's best.

Reading books is fun for Chloe,

During the day or at night.

Chloe and Sam get comfortable

While mom reads stories by flashlight.

Chloe gets cuddles and tucked in,

She finds it hard to be too sad.

Sam can sleep near her bed all night,

And she's loved by her mom and dad.

Now that they're cozy in her bed,

Chloe and Sam can have sweet dreams.

Tomorrow is sure to be filled

With adventure and friendship it seems.

Chloe and Sam
are going to bed

Fun adventure story for
children about little girl
Chloe and her dog Sam

CPSIA information can be obtained
at www.ICGtesting.com
Printed in the USA
BVHW021145031220
594824BV00016B/61

9 781986 084796